privacy in the
ONLINE WORLD

Online Privacy and Government

Harry Henderson

ReferencePoint
Press®

San Diego, CA

About the Author

Harry Henderson has written more than thirty books on computing, science, technology, and social issues. He lives with his wife, Lisa Yount (a retired writer and active artist), in El Cerrito, California.

© 2015 ReferencePoint Press, Inc.
Printed in the United States

For more information, contact:
ReferencePoint Press, Inc.
PO Box 27779
San Diego, CA 92198
www.ReferencePointPress.com

Picture Credits
Cover: Thinkstock Images; Maury Aaseng: 6; © Jim Bennett/Corbis: 27; © Bettmann/Corbis: 16; © Brian Blano/AP/Corbis: 51; © Corbis: 10; © izmostock/Izma/Corbis: 41; Natan Dvir/Newscom: 47; © Brooks Kraft/Corbis: 38; © Ron Sachs/Corbis: 57; © Paul Sakuma/AP/Corbis: 63; © Mike Simons/Corbis: 22; © Elaine Thompson/AP/Corbis: 35

LIBRARY OF CONGRESS CATALOGING-IN-PUBLICATION DATA

Henderson, Harry, 1951–
    Online privacy and government / by Harry Henderson.
        pages cm. — (Privacy in the online world)
    Includes bibliographical references and index.
    Audience: Grade 9 to 12.
    ISBN-13: 978-1-60152-726-4 (hardback)
    ISBN-10: 1-60152-726-8 (hardback)
    1. Privacy, Right of—United States—Juvenile literature. 2. Internet—Security measures—United States—Juvenile literature. 3. Data protection—United States—Juvenile literature. 4. Computer security—United States—Juvenile literature. 5. War on Terrorism, 2001–2009—Juvenile literature. I. Title.
    JC599.U5H357 2015
    323.44'802854678--dc23
                                                                    2014010964

Contents

A Shifting Balance

In the years following the terrorist attacks of September 11, 2001, government surveillance and data-gathering activities reached unprecedented levels and penetrated into virtually every form of communications or online interaction. The authority given to the executive branch by the USA PATRIOT Act of 2001 placed much of this activity outside the normal legal process, where two sides can contest an issue in open court. The secret, classified status of the new programs largely shielded them from public and even congressional scrutiny—that is, until June 5, 2013.

That was the day Edward Snowden, with the cooperation of several major media outlets, began to disclose classified documents revealing the existence of previously unknown and far-reaching surveillance programs. Snowden, a thirty-year-old system administrator employed by a contractor for the National Security Agency (NSA), said he worried that government spying threatens democracy. He insisted that

> my sole motive is to inform the public as to that which is done in their name and that which is done against them . . . because I can't in good conscience allow the US government to destroy privacy, internet freedom and basic liberties for people around the world with this massive surveillance machine they're secretly building.
>
> I don't see myself as a hero, because what I'm doing is self-interested: I don't want to live in a world where there's no privacy and therefore no room for intellectual exploration and creativity.[1]

What Snowden's disclosures eventually revealed was that the NSA, along with foreign counterparts such as the British Government Communications Headquarters (GCHQ), have for at least a decade been recording phone numbers, call times, and in some cases the contents of billions of phone calls as well as e-mails, text messages, online search queries, and even video chats.

As the months passed and the revelations continued, public opinion showed mixed views toward both Snowden and the disclosures. In a January 2014 CBS News poll, 54 percent of respondents said they disapproved of Snowden's actions, as opposed to 31 percent who supported them. However, 41 percent of respondents thought the government had gone too far in infringing on people's privacy in its efforts to fight terrorism, whereas 43 percent thought the balance was about right, and 12 percent believed the government had not gone far enough.

> "I don't want to live in a world where there's no privacy and therefore no room for intellectual exploration and creativity."[1]
>
> —*Edward Snowden, NSA whistle-blower.*

While condemning the leaking of classified information, in January 2014 President Barack Obama acknowledged public concern about the surveillance of people's communications and other online activity. The president noted that "the combination of increased digital information and powerful supercomputers offers intelligence agencies the possibility of sifting through massive amounts of bulk data to identify patterns or pursue leads that may thwart impending threats. It's a powerful tool. But the government collection and storage of such bulk data also creates a potential for abuse."[2]

The president also made a broader point about how the secrecy that is necessary for effective intelligence work makes regulating and setting appropriate limits on surveillance and data gathering more difficult. He said:

> Intelligence agencies cannot function without secrecy, which makes their work less subject to public debate. Yet there is an inevitable bias not only within the intelligence community, but among all of us who are responsible for national security,

to collect more information about the world, not less. So in the absence of institutional requirements for regular debate—and oversight that is public, as well as private or classified—the danger of government overreach becomes more acute. And this is particularly true when surveillance technology and our reliance on digital information is evolving much faster than our laws.[3]

What Online Information Should the Individual Control?

A poll conducted by the Pew Research Center in mid-2013 (just after the first revelations by Edward Snowden) suggested that many people want the ability to control who has access to certain kinds of online information.

Type of Information	Percent who say it is "very important" to have control
Content of your e-mail	68%
Whom you exchange e-mail with	62%
Content / files you download	55%
Where you are located when you use Internet	54%
Content of your online chats / hangouts	51%
Websites you browse	46%
Searches you perform	44%
Apps or programs you use	40%
Times of day you are online	33%

Source: Pew Research Center's Internet & American Life Project Omnibus Survey, conducted July 11–14, 2013. http://pewinternet.org.

A Pervasive Concern

The most prominent debate at present is about the intelligence community and the fight against terrorism. Yet the impact of surveillance, data-gathering, and data-analysis programs is now felt at all levels of government, including local police agencies and even schools. Just about every activity of daily life is potential fodder for these programs. If one sends an e-mail or a text message, it can be intercepted from the data cables connecting Google, Yahoo, or Apple to the Internet. What one posts on a Facebook page or on Twitter may be intended only for friends, but it too might become part of a detailed profile that describes an individual's activities, social connections, interests, and even beliefs.

Privacy is not just a concern when people go online. Indeed, most people are now online all of the time. The smartphone that can provide real-time traffic information or locate the nearest pizza place in the neighborhood is constantly broadcasting its location. Along with images from surveillance cameras, license plate scanners, and other sensors, virtually all activity in public spaces can be monitored.

"In the absence of institutional requirements for regular debate—and oversight that is public, as well as private or classified—the danger of government overreach becomes more acute."[3]

—US president Barack Obama, January 2014.

There are several overarching themes that can help make sense of today's online privacy issues. Social expectations of privacy have expanded as society has broadened its view of individual rights. On the other hand, willingness to tolerate intrusions on privacy has sometimes increased as concerns about crime and terrorism have grown. There is usually a considerable delay as courts and legislators attempt to fit these shifting expectations into the existing legal framework. Meanwhile, the evolution of communications and information technology, from the telephone to the Internet and mobile devices, continually poses new challenges to policy makers. Finally, many of the same technologies—and thus the same privacy issues—will be found at all levels of government, from national security and federal law enforcement agencies to local police and even schools.

Chapter 1

Privacy and the Challenge of Technology

The Eighteenth Amendment to the Constitution, passed in 1920 during the period known as the Roaring Twenties, forbade the manufacture, sale, and transport of alcoholic beverages. However, millions of Americans still wanted to drink, and their thirst fueled a vast expansion of organized crime. Police organized squads to pursue bootleggers. One suspected bootlegger was Roy Olmstead, a former policeman operating in the Seattle area.

In order to try to trace Olmstead's activities, the police wiretapped his phones for several months. Using the evidence gathered, prosecutors won convictions of Olmstead and numerous associates. However, Olmstead appealed the conviction, arguing that because the wiretapping had been done without a warrant, it violated the right of privacy as implied by the Fourth Amendment to the US Constitution. Although Olmstead lost his appeal, the issues it raised would eventually lead to a series of landmark Supreme Court decisions— and would continue to challenge courts today.

But what did "the right of privacy" mean when the Constitution was written in the 1790s? What did it mean when bootleggers' phones were tapped in the 1920s? And what might it mean today when millions of people exchange information online every hour of the day? Legal concepts and public expectations of privacy have changed over the past two centuries. These changes are driven both by the development of new technologies and changes in the priorities of government.

Privacy and the Constitution

Long before the Internet or even the telephone, privacy was about homes and their physical contents. The eighteenth-century British statesman William Pitt declared in a speech to Parliament: "The poorest man may, in his cottage, bid defiance to all the forces of the Crown. It may be frail, its roof may shake, the wind may blow through it; the storm may enter; the rain may enter; but the King of England may not enter; all his force dares not cross the threshold of the ruined tenement."[4]

Even in eighteenth-century Britain, to enter a home or business in search of evidence, officers were supposed to get a warrant signed by a judge. In a time before electronic communication, information existed only in the form of letters, diaries, ledgers, or other papers. The only way the government could get at such information would be by securing it physically. Many of the colonists who came to America from England shared this belief in the sanctity of one's home. By the middle of the eighteenth century, however, American colonists were complaining that British officers were entering homes and businesses armed only with a "general warrant" or a "writ of assistance" that did not specify what they were looking for. These arguably illegal invasions of privacy would have a considerable effect on American concerns about overly intrusive government. The Supreme Court noted in 1886 that "writs of assistance . . . were fresh in the memories of those who achieved our independence and established our form of government."[5]

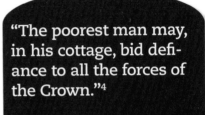

"The poorest man may, in his cottage, bid defiance to all the forces of the Crown."[4]

—*William Pitt, eighteenth-century British statesman.*

Thus, having secured independence by the 1780s, the new nation's political debate turned to the proposed Constitution and the question of how to guarantee that any future government would not infringe on individual rights. Those who argued that it was necessary to specify a Bill of Rights to explicitly limit government actions prevailed. One of its provisions, the Fourth Amendment, which provides a guarantee of protection against abusive searches or seizures, reads: "The right of the people to be secure in their persons, houses, papers, and effects, against unreasonable searches and seizures, shall not be violated, and no warrants shall issue, but upon probable cause supported by oath or affirmation, and particularly describing the place to be searched, and the persons or things to be seized."

This meant that if the police wanted to search someone's home or place of business, they would have to swear before a judge that they had "probable cause," defined by the Supreme Court as "reasonably trustworthy information" that would "warrant a man of reasonable caution in the belief that an offense has been or is being committed."[6] The police would have to specify what relevant evidence they were looking for. For example, if a business was suspected of tax fraud, the warrant might specify bookkeeping or bank records kept in an office.

Privacy in the Industrial Age

By the late nineteenth century, an extensive network of railroads linked American cities. The telegraph went along with the rails, allowing the large corporations that came to dominate manufacturing

Whiskey is poured down a sewer during Prohibition. To combat the bootlegging spawned by the alcohol ban, police tried many tactics including wiretapping phones without a warrant. This action eventually sparked debate about the right to privacy.

to coordinate their operations. The operation of these new enterprises also required keeping extensive records. The government, too, wanted more information about where people lived and how they worked. By the 1890s the first information-processing machines, mechanical punch-card sorters, came into use for the US Census and within large corporations.

However, the legal status of all this information and what happened when the government wanted to see it was not clear. For some legal writers, the growing complexity and scope of an industrial society seemed to threaten the right to go about one's daily life without unwanted intrusions. In a very influential 1890 law journal article, prominent attorney Samuel D. Warren and later Supreme Court justice Louis Brandeis noted, "The intensity and complexity of life, attendant upon advancing civilization, have rendered necessary some retreat from the world . . . so that solitude and privacy have become more essential to the individual; but modern enterprise and invention, through invasions upon his privacy, subjected him to mental pain and distress."[7] Among the troubling inventions cited by Warren and Brandeis were new high-speed printing presses that could spread sensational journalism and cameras that could take quick, candid snapshots.

Tapping the Telephone

By the 1920s many homes and businesses had phones. With more and more business being done on the phone, the question of whether the police could tap Olmstead's line thus had considerable importance. When the case got to the Supreme Court in 1928, the majority of the justices rejected Olmstead's appeal. They ruled that the Fourth Amendment only prohibited physically entering someone's property and seizing evidence without a warrant. The wiretappers had never entered Olmstead's property—they had simply put their taps on the outside phone lines.

One of the justices hearing the case was the same Louis Brandeis who had worried decades earlier about a growing assault on privacy in modern society. Brandeis could not accept the majority's narrow view of privacy protection. He argued that if the intent of the Constitution to protect personal privacy is to be maintained, the law must keep up with technology. In his 1928 opinion, he wrote: "Subtler and more far-reaching means of invading privacy have become available to the Government. Discovery and invention have made it possible for the Government, by means far more effective than stretching upon the rack, to obtain disclosure in court of what is whispered in the closet."[8]

Brandeis argued that the right of privacy had to be treated broadly in order to be true to the vision of the framers of the Constitution. "The makers of our Constitution . . . sought to protect Americans in their beliefs, their thoughts, their emotions and their sensations," he wrote. "They conferred, as against the Government, the right to be left alone—the most comprehensive of the rights of man and the right most valued by civilized men."[9] Brandeis was in the minority, however, so telephones continued to be tapped without a warrant.

> "Discovery and invention have made it possible for the Government, by means far more effective than stretching upon the rack, to obtain disclosure in court of what is whispered in the closet."[8]
>
> —*Supreme Court Justice Louis Brandeis, dissent in* Olmstead v. United States *(1928).*

An Expanding Concept of Privacy

By the 1960s society was rapidly changing, and more liberal points of view were starting to take hold in society and even in the courts. It was in this atmosphere that in 1967 the question of whether wiretapping required a warrant would be revisited. When federal agents suspected Charles Katz of running an extensive bookmaking (gambling) operation, they attached a "bug" to the outside of a phone booth he was using. They used its recording to help convict him. When he appealed, the appeals courts upheld the conviction, citing the *Olmstead* precedent and noting that the bug had been put on the outside of the booth. Olmstead's appeal eventually made it to the Supreme Court. This was a much more liberal Supreme Court under Chief Justice Earl Warren, and it was more inclined to give a broad interpretation to constitutional protections of all sorts. In its majority decision, the court declared that "the Fourth Amendment protects people, not places. What a person knowingly exposes to the public, even in his

Privacy and Freedom of Association

In 1958 the Supreme Court ruled that it was unconstitutional under the First and Fourteenth Amendments for the state of Alabama to demand that the National Association for the Advancement of Colored People turn over its membership records. The court noted that it "has recognized the vital relationship between freedom to associate and privacy in one's associations. . . . Inviolability of privacy in group association may in many circumstances be indispensable to preservation of freedom of association, particularly where a group espouses dissident beliefs."

Might the mass gathering of data by the government about people and their activities have a similar effect? In July 2013 the First Unitarian Church of Los Angeles and twenty-three other groups brought a federal suit against the NSA and the FBI. The suit claims that the collection of data from phone calls and e-mails is making people afraid to communicate or work with the groups for fear they might become the target of a government investigation. This in turn hampers the groups' ability to exercise their First Amendment right to "peaceably assemble and petition the government for redress of grievances."

Regardless of the case's outcome, the issues raised are an important part of the privacy debate. Might unchecked surveillance threaten the freedom of expression and robust debate necessary for a healthy democracy? Much will depend on the extent to which courts are willing to consider the First Amendment implications of a climate of pervasive surveillance.

National Association for the Advancement of Colored People v. Alabama, 357 US 449 (1958).

own home or office, is not a subject of Fourth Amendment protection. . . . But what he seeks to preserve as private, even in an area accessible to the public, may be constitutionally protected."[10]

One implication of this new approach would be that it would no longer be necessary for government agents to physically enter a building for a privacy violation to occur. The court declared that there would be a twofold test to determine a violation of the Fourth Amendment: first, that a person has "exhibited an actual (subjective) expectation of privacy," and second, that "the expectation be one that society is prepared to recognize as 'reasonable.'"[11]

Information Privacy

The *Katz* case established that a warrant would be required for tapping a phone line or for certain kinds of tracking or surveillance. However, tapping communications was not the only way the government might obtain information that people might reasonably expect to be private. For billing purposes, telephone companies have to keep track of each number a person calls. Similarly, banks must keep track of every check written or deposit made. It was unclear whether a warrant was required to obtain such transactional records, and eventually the Supreme Court would have to decide the issue.

> "The Fourth Amendment protects people, not places."[10]
>
> —*US Supreme Court in* Katz v. United States *(1967).*

This issue arose in 1975. After Patricia McDonough was robbed that year, she began receiving threatening and obscene phone calls from a man who said he was the robber. With the cooperation of the phone company, the police then used a device called a pen register to record all phone numbers dialed by their suspect, whom they had identified as Michael Lee Smith. Based on the register recording of McDonough's number being called by Smith, as well as other evidence, the police then obtained a search warrant and found more evidence in Smith's home.

After Smith was convicted, he appealed, claiming that the use of the pen register without a warrant violated the Fourth Amendment. When the case reached the Supreme Court in 1979, the justices considered whether Smith could reasonably expect that the fact he had called a particular phone number would be kept private. The court said no—after all, the phone company has to record the numbers one calls for billing purposes, as well as for detecting fraud and troubleshooting technical problems. In the 1976 case *United States v. Miller*, the court applied the same reasoning to the information that had to be routinely supplied to banks in order to process transactions.

What became known as the "third-party doctrine" states that information disclosed to a third party (such as a phone company or a bank) in the normal course of business does not have an expectation of privacy. But does the fact one has to give information for one purpose mean that it is now up for grabs for all purposes? Two legal scholars, Susan W. Brenner and Leo L. Clarke, do not think so. They do not believe that "disclosure to a trusted, reputable [third party] is the same as indiscriminate disclosure to the public." If one posts information on a public website, they write, "we have demonstrated our lack of interest in controlling access to the information in question." However, sharing information needed to deal with one's bank or phone company involves "controlled disclosures, in that they represent the limited, focused sharing of information with a [third party] as an integral part of a legitimate transaction."[12]

Domestic Spying and New Privacy Laws

Even as privacy rights were expanded to a limited extent in the 1960s and 1970s, the Cold War between the United States and the Soviet Union led to new government surveillance and other activities that would raise privacy questions. The FBI had as one of its tasks the detection and thwarting of foreign spies and subversive organizations working within the United States. Just what counted as subversive was subject to dispute, however. The civil rights movement and the social unrest of the 1960s and early 1970s was seen by longtime FBI director J. Edgar Hoover as being a threat to national security. The FBI had begun the Counter Intelligence Program (COINTELPRO) in the 1950s, targeting mainly the American Communist Party. However, in the 1960s COINTELPRO went beyond mere intelligence gathering to try to infiltrate and disrupt a wide array of civil rights, socialist, New Left, black nationalist, and other groups. Its tactics included planting false stories to discredit group leaders, provoking violent escalation of protests, and encouraging police harassment.

FBI director J. Edgar Hoover (pictured in 1947) viewed the civil rights movement and the social unrest that began in the 1960s as a threat to national security. Under Hoover, the FBI infiltrated and disrupted organizations involved in these causes.

In response to revelations and concerns about FBI activities, a congressional committee headed by Senator Frank Church held hearings in 1975 and considered ways to prevent future abuses. The committee observed, "Too many people have been spied upon by too many Government agencies and too much information has been collected.... The Government ... has swept in vast amounts of information about the personal lives, views, and associations of American citizens."[13]

The committee noted that this activity also posed a threat to First Amendment rights of free speech, press, and assembly: "The Government has often undertaken the secret surveillance of citizens on the basis of their political beliefs, even when those beliefs posed no threat of violence or illegal acts on behalf of a hostile foreign power."[14]

Several important privacy laws were soon passed. The Privacy Act of 1974 provided the right to examine one's government records and correct errors. The Family Educational Rights and Privacy Act of 1974 gave parents similar rights with regard to their children's school records. The Right to Financial Privacy Act of 1978 required police to get a warrant or subpoena before obtaining financial records. During the 1980s additional laws extended privacy protections to cable TV accounts, government searches of databases, video purchase records, and driver's license information.

Legal scholar Marc Rotenberg notes that this series of laws brought together two ideas: restrictions on government information-gathering activities and the need to inform the public about what the government was doing. He writes:

"Too many people have been spied upon by too many Government agencies and too much information has been collected. . . . The Government . . . has swept in vast amounts of information about the personal lives, views, and associations of American citizens."[13]

—*Report of the Church Committee, 1976.*

In enacting both the Privacy Act of 1974 and adopting the amendments that same year which significantly strengthened the Freedom of Information Act, Congress sought to ensure that personal information collected and maintained by federal agencies would be properly protected while also seeking to ensure that public information in the possession of federal agencies would be widely available to the public. The complementary goals of safeguarding individual liberty and ensuring government accountability were enabled by legislation that protected privacy on the one hand and promoted government oversight on the other.[15]

Government Databases and Electronic Privacy

Computer databases kept by government agencies were growing by the 1970s. This raised the questions of whom this information might be shared with and what would happen if information was not accurate. What seemed to be needed was a set of agreed-upon standards that would be adopted by all agencies. A 1973 report by the US Department

17

Spying on the Spies

In the early 1970s the FBI conducted a massive surveillance and harassment program called COINTELPRO; it focused on political dissidents and radicals. In these predigital days the data the FBI compiled filled many drawers of paper file folders. A small band of activists decided to turn the tables on the government agents. As one of them, Keith Forsyth, recalled later, "When you talked to people outside the movement about what the F.B.I. was doing, nobody wanted to believe it. There was only one way to convince people it was true, and that was to get it in their handwriting."

Forsyth and seven other activists decided to break in to an FBI office in Media, Pennsylvania, to look for evidence of the agency's spying and harassment of antiwar groups and others. They carefully cased the building, watching agents' daily routines, and got one member to visit it by posing as a job seeker. On the night of March 8, 1971, they broke into the office and packed the files into suitcases, filling several cars. They then passed selected documents to journalists at newspapers such as the *Washington Post* and the *New York Times*. The articles that resulted helped arouse the public concern that eventually led to the investigation of FBI activities by a committee headed by Senator Frank Church of Idaho.

The burglars were never caught, but in 2014 journalist Betty Medsger revealed their story in a book titled *The Burglary: The Discovery of J. Edgar Hoover's Secret FBI.*

Quoted in Mark Mazzetti, "Burglars Who Took on F.B.I. Abandon Shadows," *New York Times*, January 7, 2014. www.nytimes.com.

of Health, Education, and Welfare moved ahead with this idea when it recommended a Code of Fair Information Practices based on five principles:

- There must be no personal data record-keeping systems whose very existence is secret.

- There must be a way for a person to find out what information about the person is in a record and how it is used.

- There must be a way for a person to prevent information about the person that was obtained for one purpose from being used or made available for other purposes without the person's consent.

- There must be a way for a person to correct or amend a record of identifiable information about the person.

- Any organization creating, maintaining, using, or disseminating records of identifiable personal data must assure the reliability of the data for their intended use and must take precautions to prevent misuses of the data.[16]

These principles were largely incorporated in the 1974 Privacy Act, but their applicability to the programs and policies of the twenty-first century would raise serious questions.

By the mid-1980s new forms of electronic communication were being used. These included faxes, pagers, tracking devices, and even early forms of e-mail and online messaging. The Electronic Communications Privacy Act of 1986 extended the protection against phone wiretapping to digital communications. However, these protections would prove to be limited. For example, e-mail stored on servers more than six months (now a common practice with services such as Gmail) could be accessed without a warrant.

Through the 1990s more and more people came online as the Internet was thrown open to public use and web browsers made it easy to access. Along with the growing use of the web for business and personal pursuits came growing concerns about the vulnerability of online users and the potential misuse of information by both private businesses and government agencies. But the terrorist attacks of September 11, 2001, and the responses that followed would soon change the rules of the game.

Chapter 2

Online Privacy and the War on Terrorism

As the twenty-first century began, government databases containing people's personal information and details of their transactions were rapidly growing. As most people would learn only after Edward Snowden's revelations, information about people's online communications, postings, and transactions was also finding its way into such databases. Exactly what information was being used and for what purposes remains unclear. However, there could be serious consequences, as one family found out.

Photojournalist and journalism professor Najlah Feanny Hicks and her two-year-old son, Michael, were trying to print their boarding pass at an airport kiosk, but the machine told them they must check in with the airline. At the counter they were told that Michael Hicks was on a list of people who were deemed to be security risks and faced heightened scrutiny. These lists (which include the no-fly list, a selectee list, and a Terrorist Screening Database) are maintained by the Terrorist Screening Center, which supplies them to the FBI and the Transportation Security Administration. Altogether the lists contain more than 1 million names. The procedures used to decide who goes on these lists are kept secret, presumably to keep would-be terrorists from getting around them.

According to Hicks, little Michael was thoroughly patted down and began to cry. Scenes like this would become the new normal for many people who have a name that is similar to a name on the list. Getting the government to determine that one is not a possible terrorist is far from easy. As of 2010, more than eighty thousand people had petitioned for such action, and more than twenty-five thousand of the petitioners were still waiting for action to be taken.

In June 2010 the American Civil Liberties Union filed a lawsuit claiming that the list process denied the right to due process guaranteed by the Fifth Amendment. The government moved for a summary judgment rejecting the claims, but in August 2013 a federal court ruled that constitutional rights were at issue and ordered both sides to provide more details.

9/11 and Expanding Government Powers

The flight lists are only one weapon in an all-out and far-reaching war on terrorism in response to the September 11, 2001, attacks. The shock in the wake of the devastation of New York City's Twin Towers, at the Pentagon in Washington, DC, and in a Pennsylvania field left the Bush administration, Congress, and indeed many Americans in no mood for careful consideration of issues such as privacy or government accountability.

Passed with virtually no debate or scrutiny, the USA PATRIOT Act of 2001 reflected a fundamental shift in priorities for federal agencies from law enforcement to homeland security and the detection and investigation of possible terrorist activity. A new agency, the US Department of Homeland Security, consolidated many previously separate agencies and took responsibility for protection of borders, transportation services (particularly airlines), and other critical facilities.

Surveillance powers were also extended or expanded in areas such as wiretapping and access to business records. Secret national security letters were increasingly used by the FBI to obtain the addresses and other identifying information (called "metadata") for e-mails and other online data without a warrant. The use of these new powers and capabilities was to be supervised by the US Foreign Intelligence Surveillance Court (FISC), which was established in 1978 in the wake of the Church Committee's hearings on intelligence abuses. As described in a 2007 legal pleading:

> The FISC is a unique court. Its entire docket relates to the collection of foreign intelligence by the federal government. The applications submitted to it by the government are clas-

sified, as are the overwhelming majority of the FISC's orders. Court sessions are held behind closed doors in a secure facility, and every proceeding in its history prior to this one has been . . . with the government the only party.[17]

Because this court's proceedings were secret, the public would not know what government programs were being questioned. Members of Congress who were on the intelligence committees of the House and Senate were given regular briefings. However, since the information was classified, they could not talk about it, and there is some question whether even these insiders were fully informed.

However, some details began to surface in 2003 about a program that was under development called Total Information Awareness (later the Terrorism Information Awareness Program). The program was intended to bring together phone records, e-mail, credit card and banking information, court records, travel documents, and other data without requiring a search warrant or designating a specific individ-

Demonstrators protest the Patriot Act during a 2003 speech by US attorney general John Ashcroft, who defended the law as necessary for safeguarding Americans. The Patriot Act, passed shortly after the 9/11 terrorist attacks, expanded government surveillance powers.

ual. According to Oregon senator Ron Wyden, the program would have been "the biggest surveillance program in the history of the United States."[18] However, Congress pushed back at the program by limiting its scope, and the Bush administration eventually dropped the idea.

This was only one of a number of shadowy surveillance and data-analysis programs, however. In 2005 the *New York Times* revealed that the NSA was routinely intercepting communications in which one party was outside the United States and the other inside the country. The Bush administration vigorously defended this Terrorist Surveillance Program. Meanwhile, several lawsuits were brought against telecommunications companies, arguing that the companies, in cooperating with the NSA, had violated surveillance laws. Many privacy advocates hoped that the lawsuits would lead to the disclosure of more details about the government's surveillance programs.

Intelligence agencies and their supporters in Congress believed that revealing such information would endanger the effort to combat terrorism. The phone companies did not believe they should be forced to defend themselves in court for actions the government had ordered them to perform. Pressure was exerted on Congress, which resulted in the phone companies being given immunity from being sued for cooperating with the intelligence agencies.

Other legal challenges ultimately went nowhere, because the court said the government could classify the very evidence needed to prove that the surveillance had taken place. Thus, the power to declare state secrets, sometimes a necessity for protecting national security, makes it nearly impossible for the subjects of government surveillance to successfully challenge that practice in court.

Snowden and Prism

From 2006 onward scattered reports about other NSA activities appeared in the media. In 2012 *Wired* magazine reported on a massive data center being built in Utah for the NSA and other intelligence agencies. According to James Bamford (who has written extensively about the history and operations of the NSA), "Flowing through its servers and routers and stored in near-bottomless databases will be all forms of communication, including the complete contents of private emails, cell phone calls, and Google searches, as well as all sorts of personal data trails—parking receipts, travel itineraries, bookstore purchases, and other digital 'pocket litter.'"[19]

Such stories aroused strong concerns by privacy advocates and followers of cybersecurity issues. By 2009, however, the Obama administration had taken over responsibility for the war on terrorism, and the sharp criticism of the Bush era had become somewhat muted.

This changed starting in June 2013 when the British newspaper the *Guardian* revealed that Verizon had handed over call logs from its giant network as part of a secret NSA program called Prism. Snowden, who was the source of this information, also said that the NSA had also scooped up phone calls and e-mails from the companies that millions of people use online every day—Google, Yahoo, Facebook, Microsoft, and Apple. Hobbled by legal restraints and their own confusion, the leading tech companies struggled to respond. For example, Google chief legal officer, David Drummond, faced comments such as these on the *Guardian* website:

> "Flowing through its servers and routers and stored in near-bottomless databases will be all forms of communication, including the complete contents of private emails, cell phone calls, and Google searches, as well as all sorts of personal data trails."[19]
>
> —*NSA historian James Bamford, describing the agency's giant new data center.*

Isn't this whole show not just a face-saving exercise . . . after you have been found to be in cahoots with the NSA?

How can we tell if Google is lying to us?

We lost a decade-long trust in you, Google.

I will cease using Google mail.[20]

What made matters worse for the companies was that the stream of Snowden's revelations appearing in the *Guardian* and other newspapers seemed unending. The whole atmosphere in which people viewed Internet privacy had been poisoned. As Michael Buckley,

Toward a Universal ID Card

Responding to concerns about border security and terrorism, Congress passed the Real ID Act in 2005. One provision required the development of uniform standards for state-issued driver's licenses and ID cards and required states to share their ID databases. However, a coalition of civil rights supporters, immigrant advocacy groups, and others vigorously opposed many of the act's provisions, and as of 2014 only about half the states have implemented the ID requirements.

The Electronic Privacy Information Center in a 2008 report suggested that Real ID might come with security problems: "The final regulations include poor privacy and security safeguards for the sensitive personal data of cardholders. . . . Technical safeguards need to be incorporated into both the identity card and the databases systems."

Of course, cards of any sort are increasingly old-fashioned. Soon many people may be carrying cell phones with radio-frequency identification or biometric fingerprint scanners built in. While more convenient for users, using these devices would create data pinpointing the identity and location of individuals. Even though the data would be held by companies such as Apple, Google, or credit card issuers, the government could still obtain it. The upshot is that while the universal ID may be a potent symbol that conjures images of pervasive government surveillance, the capability of identifying anyone anywhere already effectively exists.

Electronic Privacy Information Center, "Real ID Implementation Review: Few Benefits, Staggering Costs," May 2008, p. 4. http://epic.org.

global head of communications for Facebook, lamented, "The fact is, the government can't put the genie back into the bottle. We can put out any statement or statistics, but in the wake of what feels like weekly disclosures of other government activity, the question is, will anyone believe us?"[21]

More Revelations

In October 2013 another Snowden leak revealed another huge government–data-collection program. In a single day, this involved 444,743 e-mail address books from Yahoo, 105,068 from Hotmail, 82,857 from Facebook, 33,697 from Gmail, and 22,881 from smaller services. Unlike the data that Prism apparently collected directly from servers, this information was apparently collected as the data flowed through the cables and fibers linking corporate data centers. This meant that the Internet communications companies had not even been aware their users' data was being collected. There was thus no opportunity for them to mount a legal challenge. Since the data was intercepted before it was stored on servers, any encryption applied there would not protect data from being read. Responding to the growing furor, Caitlin Hayden, spokesperson for Obama's National Security Council, says that the president "believes that there are steps we can take to give the American people additional confidence that there are added safeguards against abuse, including putting in place greater oversight, greater transparency, and further constraints on the use of this authority."[22]

> "The fact is, the government can't put the genie back into the bottle."[21]
>
> —*Michael Buckley, Facebook executive, responding to revelations of government surveillance.*

Why did the government want to collect as much information as possible from phone calls and online communications? The simplest answer was to put software to work looking for key words or phrases that might indicate terrorist activity or intentions or that might help pinpoint the location of terrorist leaders or cells of operatives. Thus, the head of the NSA, former army general Keith Alexander, defended the Prism program, saying it enables "the NSA to see threats from Afghanistan and Pakistan and around the world, share those insights with the FBI—who can look inside the United States, based on their authorities—and find out, is there something bad going to happen here?"[23]

As an example of this intelligence cooperation, Alexander cited the case of Najibullah Zazi, a radical Islamist who had planned to bomb the New York subway in 2009. Alexander suggested that information collected by Prism had been passed to the FBI, which helped the agency capture Zazi and prevent the bombing.

Edward Snowden (pictured in 2014) publicly revealed several secret government–data-collection programs. Some of these programs involved phone and e-mail records from major Internet and computer companies.

Describing Prism and other programs as having stirred up a "hornet's nest" of opposition, Alexander said that as much as he would like to get rid of such programs, "if we do that, our nation now is at greater risk for a terrorist attack. So we're going to do the right thing; we're going to hold onto it, let people look at the options. If there is a better option, put it on the table."[24]

How Effective Are the Programs?

Proponents of mass data-gathering programs point to the potential of using increasingly sophisticated software to find patterns in the data that point to possible terrorist activities. After all, one of the failures that led to the success of the 9/11 attack was the failure to spot connections between the partially and sporadically observed activities of some of the hijackers. Computers, however, are good at searching through vast haystacks of data for possible needles. The machines never get distracted, become tired, or get embroiled in rivalries with other agencies.

27

While defenders point to successes for the new surveillance programs, critics such as analysts from the New America Foundation, a nonpartisan public policy think tank, suggest that what evidence is publicly available about actual incidents does not support the effectiveness of the mass surveillance and data-gathering programs. It says, "Surveillance of American phone metadata has had no discernible impact on preventing acts of terrorism and only the most marginal of impacts on preventing terrorist-related activity, such as fundraising for a terrorist group."[25]

Data Mining

The process of deriving useful information from masses of data is called data mining. In the world of commerce, data mining is so important that it forms a major part of the business plans of the most successful online companies. Google, Amazon, and Facebook depend on knowing as much about their users as possible in order to either sell them products and services directly or sell advertisers access to users. All this online activity joins with communications in the great stream of data that can be tapped in various ways by intelligence agencies. As Daniel J. Solove, a prominent law professor and writer on digital privacy issues, observes: "With a complete listing of IP addresses, the government can learn quite a bit about a person because it can trace how that person surfs the Internet. . . . URLs can reveal the specific information that people are viewing on the Web. URLs can also contain search terms."[26]

> "If we [end Prism] our nation now is at greater risk for a terrorist attack. So we're going to do the right thing; we're going to hold onto it, let people look at the options. If there is a better option, put it on the table."[24]
>
> —*General Keith Alexander, NSA head.*

Data mining techniques can be used in two different ways by investigators. If a government agency already has some evidence that suggests a particular individual may be engaged in terrorist or criminal activity, analysts can focus on obtaining as much information about that person as possible. Depending on the type of information sought, obtaining it may require getting a warrant.

The Revelations Continue

In February 2014 yet another secret surveillance program was exposed through documents supplied by Edward Snowden. The *Guardian* revealed that GCHQ, the British national communications intelligence agency, had intercepted millions of webcam images from Yahoo online video chats from at least 2008 to 2012. In a program called Optic Nerve, the British agency, with the cooperation of the NSA, tapped directly into Internet cables to sample images from online chats. GCHQ also experimented with automatic searching and identification of individuals based on facial recognition software. With the proper software, a database of pictures and identifying information could be continuously compiled.

If there were a terrorist attack, images from nearby cameras could be compared against the database to identify potential suspects or witnesses. However, such a database might as easily be used for more dubious purposes, such as identifying antigovernment protesters. Yahoo objected strenuously when it learned about the surveillance program: "This report, if true, represents a whole new level of violation of our users' privacy that is completely unacceptable."

Quoted in Spencer Ackerman and James Ball, "Optic Nerve: Yahoo Webcam Images from Millions of Users Intercepted by GCHQ," *Guardian* (London), February 27, 2014. www.theguardian.com.

The problem for investigators is that terrorists may well be operating in secret, undetected by agents or informants until their plots are well advanced, or worse, until a bomb goes off. It would be impossible for agents to directly examine the vast flow of information being generated by today's digital commerce and online communications. However, software can be programmed to sift through the river of data for information that fits a variety of patterns. As Solove notes:

> With the new information supplied by the private sector, there
> is an increased potential for more automated investigations,

such as searches for all people who purchase books about particular topics or those who visit certain websites, or perhaps even people whose personal interests fit a profile for those likely to engage in certain forms of criminal activity. . . . Profiles can be based on stereotypes, race, or religion. A profile is only as good as its designer. Profiles are often kept secret, enabling prejudices and faulty assumptions to exist unchecked by the public.[27]

> "Surveillance of American phone metadata has had no discernible impact on preventing acts of terrorism and only the most marginal of impacts on preventing terrorist-related activity."[25]
>
> —*Report from the New America Foundation.*

Automated investigations might identify suspects who otherwise might have gone unnoticed and free to carry out attacks. However, as another legal writer, Daniel J. Steinbock, notes, there is the problem of what to do about targeting people who turn out to be innocent of any wrongdoing: "Errors in the data will produce a larger number of falsely positive results, thereby imposing unnecessary harms. This effectively externalizes the error costs of the computer-generated decision onto its subjects."[28] Steinbock is also concerned that when individuals are matched by computers to profiles, there are usually no procedures in place to allow them to challenge the accuracy of the data or the decision process used.

Widening Consequences

The issue of privacy is not just about the ability of individuals to control what happens to their information. The techniques used to obtain information may have serious consequences for international relations, the global economy, and even the Internet itself.

When it was revealed in 2013 that the calls or e-mails of world leaders such as German chancellor Angela Merkel had been scooped up by the NSA's surveillance programs, the result was expressions of outrage, particularly in Europe. The majority of customers for America's most successful Internet-based companies actually live outside the United States. What if they stopped using services such as Gmail, Yahoo, or Facebook in favor of homegrown alternatives? American companies might lose much of their revenue, as well as access to some of the fastest-growing markets. Security-conscious nations, particularly in Europe where privacy laws are often stricter than in the United States, might require that data they generate not be transmitted beyond their borders. They might even set up separate networks. The World Wide Web might become fragmented into national or regional webs and networks. As a result, the Internet might lose much of its value as a global information highway. Even if the necessity for global communications and commerce prevents such fragmentation, the existence of new, more stringent regulations in some countries may add costly complexity to operating online businesses.

Surveillance and Internet Security

Another unanswered question is the extent to which government actions in the name of national security may actually be undermining everyone's online security. According to cryptography expert Whitfield Diffie:

> On balance we are better off with a secure computer infrastructure than with one that builds surveillance into the network fabric. At times this might press law enforcement to exercise more initiative and imagination in its investigations. On the other hand, in a society completely dependent on computer-to-computer communications, the alternative presents a hazard whose dimensions are as yet impossible to comprehend.[29]

An additional concern involves the reliability of encryption. Encryption attempts to make data unreadable to anyone who does not have the proper "key." One of the assignments given to the NSA has been to develop strong (hard-to-crack) encryption procedures to help protect sensitive business information (such as the designs of new products). In 2013, however, reports in the *New York Times* and other

31

publications based on documents disclosed by Snowden suggested that for a number of years, "the agency has circumvented or cracked much of the encryption, or digital scrambling, that guards global commerce and banking systems, protects sensitive data like trade secrets and medical records, and automatically secures the e-mails, Web searches, Internet chats and phone calls of Americans and others around the world."[30]

The extent to which the encryption relied on by most users has been compromised remains unclear. The actual encryption algorithms, which use well-understood mathematical principles, remain very hard to crack. Much depends on whether the computers, data routers, and other infrastructure involving a given source of data may have been compromised, such as by installing hardware or software that could intercept data before it can be encrypted. Nevertheless, tech journalist Quinn Norton points out some potentially serious unintended consequences of the NSA's alleged weakening of cryptographic systems: "Hostile governments, organized crime, hacking groups for hire, or even quiet bands of malevolent mathematicians can and probably have found these weaknesses, compromising the security of innocent people whom the NSA has no interest in, or in protecting. This crypto doesn't just protect banks. It protects medical records, shipping, travel, and all kinds of critical infrastructure the world over."[31]

Thus, the measures taken in the name of improving intelligence capability for national security might actually undermine the security of the systems that the nation's economic well-being depends on. As the long-term consequences of mass data gathering continue to ripple, the impact on domestic American politics remains uncertain. Well into the second decade after 9/11, with Osama bin Laden gone and the US military involvement in Iraq and Afghanistan winding down, the war on terrorism has become less of a crusade and more of an institution. Despite public concern about surveillance, calls for congressional investigation, and reforms proposed by the Obama administration, it was unclear by 2014 whether a new balance would be struck between protecting privacy and forestalling the terrorist threat.

Chapter 3

Online Privacy and Law Enforcement

Today, in addition to all the modern tools of forensics that enable the analysis of fingerprints, footprints, or trace evidence in the physical world, police are increasingly uncovering the lives of victims and the trails of suspects across the digital landscape of social media. When they identify persons of interest, police specialists look for Facebook pages, Twitter feeds, Craigslist ads, and other signs of online activity.

In December 2010, when police found four bodies in the brush along Ocean Parkway in Long Island and were able to identify them, they believed they were likely victims of the same serial killer. Searching online, they discovered the four female victims had something in common. They were all prostitutes who had advertised their services on Craigslist, the popular online service that has largely replaced personal ads in newspaper classified sections.

Boston police also use a variety of online sources to investigate killings. When they discovered that one woman who had been killed and another who had been attacked had both advertised massage services on Craigslist, they used a subpoena to get computer and phone records to identify a suspect who had communicated with both women. When they needed a photo for the wanted bulletin, they only had to go to the suspect's Facebook page.

Social network services such as Facebook can be quite useful for tracking down criminals. Of course, sometimes the suspect helps out, as in the case of Maxi Sopo, who was wanted for bank fraud in 2009 and posted a running account on Facebook of how much fun he was having with his money. Although Sopo's Facebook profile was private, his list of friends was not. By working through the list of friends, the FBI was able to track Sopo down and have him extradited from Mexico to face trial.

Police Patrol Online

In cases like the ones in Long Island or Boston, investigators went online because existing physical evidence suggested they could learn more about the suspects or victims by going on the web. As with federal analysts going after specific terrorism suspects, the potential privacy issues are relatively straightforward. Generally, what people put on their public pages on services such as Facebook is available to investigators without a warrant. However, to get access to everything a suspect has posted, including postings restricted to friends, Facebook requires that a subpoena or search warrant be presented. In other words, the rules specified in the Fourth Amendment as interpreted by the courts come into play.

Increasingly, however, the online world has become like a regular police patrol beat in cyberspace. Just as cops drive around neighborhoods looking for potential trouble, police (often specially trained) can examine web searches and links or follow social networks in an attempt to find signs of crime. John F. Timoney, who served as first deputy police commissioner in New York and earlier as Miami's chief of police, suggested that one reason police are now so interested in the online world is because the criminals they are seeking spend a lot of time there as well. As Timoney states, "In my time, in the last decade, [the Internet] has become increasingly of greater assistance to law enforcement. In the old days, the flim-flam might have been in front of a bank, or grocery store, where you met the person, where the beginnings of the crime took place. And now it's on Craigslist."[32]

> "In the old days, the flim-flam might have been in front of a bank, or grocery store, where you met the person, where the beginnings of the crime took place. And now it's on Craigslist."[32]
>
> —John F. Timoney, former New York deputy police commissioner.

This kind of open-ended monitoring activity has become fairly routine. By 2009 a *New York Times* editorial noted that "the government is increasingly monitoring Facebook, Twitter and other social networking sites for tax delinquents, copyright infringers and political protesters."[33] Around the same time, *The Wall Street Journal* reported that state tax agents had begun

Police tracked down Maxi Sopo (pictured on his Facebook page) thanks to his posts detailing his spending spree with money allegedly obtained through bank fraud. Police agencies have found social media sites to be useful investigative tools.

looking for tax violators by examining information on Facebook and Myspace pages.

Some liken law enforcement surveillance of this sort to the NSA mass data collection in that it applies to both innocent and potentially guilty social network users. Even if restricted to public postings, knowing that police may be reading one's pages with potential criminal charges in mind may feel disturbing or creepy. A known, heavy police presence might also dampen the enthusiasm of those who might want to exercise their First Amendment rights—such as by criticizing the actions of the police.

Undercover and Online

News reports of undercover operations on social networking sites have also raised concerns. Michael D. Silva, a legal advisor to the Tucson police department, reports that four out of five police agencies

35

surveyed use social networking as an investigative tool. The *Boston Globe*, citing comments from a Massachusetts district attorney, has reported that police are going undercover on Facebook.

Undercover operations, such as a sting in which police seek to buy drugs or engage prostitutes, are nothing new. If properly supervised, undercover agents can be effective in discovering and thwarting more serious crimes, such as racketeering, political corruption, or murder for hire. However, Silva suggests that the use of online services by undercover police can raise troubling issues. As noted earlier, if police want to access information on Facebook that is private or restricted to certain friends, they must get a warrant. But what if an undercover agent tricks someone into friending him or her, giving the agent access to the person's private postings? Or the agent tricks one of a person's existing friends into sharing information? Silva notes that these things can be easy to do, and there are often few or no rules in place to regulate when and how such an online masquerade is performed:

> Any law enforcement officer, regardless of experience level or assignment, with a little motivation, a laptop, and Internet access can embark on a social network–based investigation by creating a fictitious online persona. With a couple dozen keystrokes, a few mouse clicks, and a picture "borrowed" from a random website, even the most junior officers could find themselves in control of a department-sponsored covert account. It is how they create that fictitious account and the manner in which they use it that are concerns. The integrity of the investigations, the security of the investigators, and the civil liability exposure of the agency hang in the balance.[34]

Silva suggests that police develop guidelines and procedures for requesting an undercover investigation, documenting the investigation in detail, and ensuring that the proper legal procedures are used for obtaining and preserving evidence.

Keeping Up with Technology

The possibility of communications surveillance began about a century ago with the widespread use of the telephone. The modern cell phone and Internet-based phone services have made things more complicated. The concept of a wire or even a phone line is pretty much meaningless when communications can be sent and received just about anywhere using devices ranging from desktop computers to tablets, smartphones, and even wearable devices such as Google Glass. The form of communications also varies greatly, from digitized voice calls to text messages, e-mails, and tweets on Twitter. Warrants are supposed to be specific, but what if the evidence being sought might be found on any of a variety of channels or services? The legal system simply is not set up to regulate such activity and protect the privacy of personal information.

Further, it is not just the contents of communications that might be of interest to investigators. The growing use of mobile devices offers opportunities for obtaining information not only in real time but in great depth. The mobile device can become a sort of window through which investigators can pursue the whole range of a person's online activity. Mark Marshall, police chief and president of the International Association of Chiefs of Police, testified in 2011:

> "The advanced features of today's phones can process more information about where people have been, who they know and are calling, what they are texting, pictures they have and are sending, as well as larger amounts of data than ever before."[35]
>
> —Mark Marshall, president of the International Association of Chiefs of Police.

> The advanced features of today's phones can process more information about where people have been, who they know and are calling, what they are texting, pictures they have and are sending, as well as larger amounts of data than ever before. Information recovered can also produce connections to other media like Facebook and Twitter, contact lists, call history, calendars, GPS waypoints, and email.
>
> If properly recovered, this sort of stored data on communication devices has great investigative and intelligence value to assist law enforcement with investigations.[35]

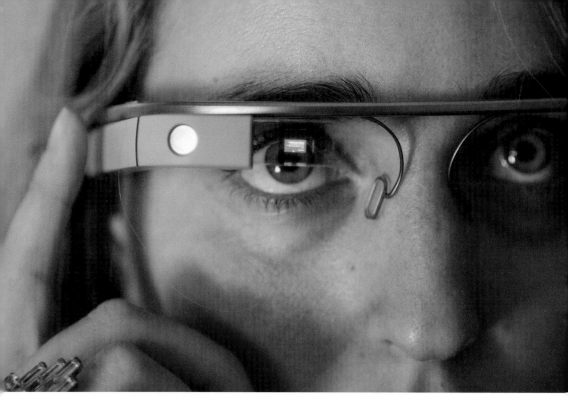

New mobile technologies such as Google Glass, the wearable mobile computer, are capable of sending and receiving information to and from just about anywhere. These mobile devices have created new privacy challenges for the legal system.

Marshall argues that technology is advancing so rapidly that police may not know how to obtain the online information they are legally authorized to pursue. He says that police are seeking better tools for monitoring the ever-changing streams of online data and social media.

The Location of Privacy

Just as phones are no longer single devices but part of a spectrum of personal communications, tracking someone is no longer a question of planting bugs or locator devices. Instead, the person's electronic communications and online activity can serve as their own bug or beacon, continually broadcasting where that person is and what they are likely to be doing. While tracking online activity can give a pretty accurate fix on a person's location, Global Positioning System (GPS) devices are even more precise. GPS is now commonly used in car navigation systems and smartphones. If police know where a person shops or whom he or she meets with regularly, they can obtain much information that may be irrelevant to a criminal investigation yet be of a sensitive personal nature. For example, suppose a person is carrying on an extramarital affair or visiting an abortion clinic or a facility that specializes in treating AIDS or another serious disease? Or suppose the person is part of a protest group?

The courts had to broaden their concept of communications privacy to extend beyond the walls of the office or phone booth. Similarly, judges are now struggling to determine what should be considered private about a person's location and activities. So far, though, the focus has been on GPS devices that have to be physically attached to a vehicle. In *United States v. Jones* (2012), the Supreme Court tried to set new ground rules for the use of GPS tracking by police. The FBI and local police had attached a GPS tracking device to a car belonging to Antoine Jones, a Washington, DC, nightclub owner and suspected leader of a major drug operation. For twenty-eight days the police knew exactly where that car went. All of the justices agreed that Jones's Fourth Amendment rights had been violated, but they disagreed by 5–4 on just what constituted the violation. Justice Antonin Scalia, writing for the majority, said that attaching the GPS device to the car was the unreasonable search.

However, two other justices wrote opinions that expressed broader concerns that seem to extend to the online world. Justice Sonia Sotomayor suggested that GPS tracking should be seen in the larger context of information that is constantly being gathered about people's daily activities. "In the course of carrying out mundane tasks, people disclose the phone numbers they dial, the URLs [web addresses] they visit . . . the books, groceries and medications they purchase."[36] In other words, someone who knows a person's physical routine and online habits would also be able to find out other important details about that person's life. It would be like assigning a fulltime plainclothes detective to follow the person.

> "In the course of carrying out mundane tasks, people disclose the phone numbers they dial, the URLs [web addresses] they visit . . . the books, groceries and medications they purchase."[36]
>
> —*Justice Sonia Sotomayor in* United States v. Jones *(2012).*

Surveillance and the Boston Bombings

April 15, 2013, was a bright afternoon in Boston, where the celebrated Boston Marathon footrace was being run. At 2:49 p.m. near the finish line, two bombs built into pressure cookers exploded and sent shards of metal flying into the runners and spectators. Three people were killed, and more than a dozen others lost limbs in the blast or later required amputations. Almost 250 people were injured in all.

The bombers were observed, however, not only by surveillance cameras in front of a store, but by cell phone video as bystanders watched their family members and friends running in the race. In a matter of hours, images of the suspects were being circulated. As *New York Times* writer Jon Healey notes, "It's a great thing when a camera meant to stop shoplifters helps police identify suspects in a terrorist attack or other brutal crime."

On the other hand, Beth Givens of the Privacy Rights Clearinghouse is worried about all the other times the cameras are running: "I'm looking ahead in horror to the day when our security cameras are equipped with facial recognition biometrics. When that day comes, there will be absolutely no anonymity in public places." The ability to identify anyone instantly would make it easy for authorities to combine it with online searches to put together a detailed profile of an individual's activities and associates.

Jon Healey, "Surveillance Cameras and the Boston Marathon Bombing," *Los Angeles Times*, April 17, 2013. http://articles.latimes.com.

With so many people now carrying smartphones, the task of the detective becomes easier. After all, who needs to attach a tracking device to someone's car when their phone is constantly communicating with several cell phone towers at a time, allowing its location to be determined rather precisely? The GPS that is built into modern smartphones can refine tracking accuracy to a matter of a few feet.

Where Law Enforcement Meets Homeland Security

The same techniques used by the NSA to pull in vast quantities of information about phone calls have also been used in federal law enforcement. In September 2013 the *New York Times* published documents revealing a program called Hemisphere. Although the full extent of the program remains unclear, a number of law enforcement agencies have apparently been given access to the records of billions of calls passing through AT&T's phone switches. No search warrant is required to access this information, only a document called an administrative subpoena, which does not require court permission. Other major phone companies declined to discuss whether they also participate in this program.

As with terrorism investigations, there are basically two ways authorities can use online data in their investigations. One is to start with a suspect who has been identified using traditional methods such

GPS devices in smartphones and cars can be used to pinpoint a person's location and patterns of activity. This capability raises concerns about unreasonable searches by law enforcement.

as forensic analysis or interviewing witnesses. They can then, as in the case of the Craigslist suspects, look for that person's online "footprint" in the form of social media postings, as well as getting a court order to look at phone records, e-mail, or text messages stored on online services. Although there can be legal disputes about whether the police followed proper procedure, this sort of online activity by police fits pretty well into an established legal framework.

Increasingly, though, police are following the lead of Homeland Security and other antiterrorism agencies. More and more they are collecting streams of broad surveillance from street cameras, license plate scanners, and other sensors and combining them with online data from a variety of sources, including social media. Some police departments are building facilities that will allow them to perform and integrate these activities in a single location. One such facility is the Domain Awareness Center being built in Oakland, California. This effort is encouraged by generous federal grants that allow otherwise cash-strapped local police agencies to obtain powerful computers, software, and new surveillance tools, even drones.

Several arguments are made in favor of these new centers. The new technology could speed police response time, such as by automatically tracking gunshots or following suspect vehicles. Closer integration with homeland security agencies could bring resources quickly to bear in response to a terrorist attack, such as the 2013 Boston Marathon bombing.

The lack of clear-cut policies describing how data would be collected and used and how privacy would be protected has aroused opposition. For example, it was not clear how long the Oakland police department kept license plate data. The Oakland police were also using a device called a stingray that could track cell phones even when they were not being used to make calls—potentially allowing for continuous monitoring of a person's location.

In a hearing, Oakland city council member Libby Schaaf noted, "It's our responsibility to take advantage of new tools that become available." However, she also admitted that with all this new technology, integration, and "big data" analysis, police would be able to "paint a pretty detailed picture of someone's personal life, someone who may be innocent."[37] Because of such privacy concerns as well as concerns

Turning the Cameras Around

One way to push back against government intrusions on privacy is to make the activities of authorities publicly visible. Many of the online tools police use to watch citizens and look for criminal activity can also be used by citizen groups that are concerned about police misconduct. In 2009 the National Association for the Advancement of Colored People set up a website and encouraged people to send video or text reports from their cell phones if they see police engaged in questionable conduct. Reporting on this development, a writer on *The Agitator* blog suggested that

> as we saw in Iran last month [June 2009], the ability to instantly capture photos and video and store them off-site is an incredibly powerful tool. As more and more people acquire it, police officers will have to approach their jobs with the knowledge that everything they do while on duty can be legally captured and stored on a server they won't be able to access. Confiscating phones and cameras won't work anymore.

The Agitator (blog), "NAACP Sets Up Site for Cell Videos of Police Misconduct," July 18, 2009. www .theagitator.com.

that police might track political protesters, opponents of the Domain Awareness Center succeeded in restricting the program to covering only the Port of Oakland (perhaps a more legitimate focus for homeland security), rather than the whole city.

Toward Workable Policies

The challenge of using appropriate new tools for law enforcement in a way that is guided by clear policies and accountable to the community is only beginning to be faced. The courts or Congress may provide guidance in some aspects of the problem, but much will depend on what each city, county, or state decides.

There is also a possible connection between what is decided about police surveillance and what intelligence agencies should be allowed to do. Legal oversight and access to the courts to resolve privacy issues involving intelligence agencies is hampered by the secrecy of their operations and perhaps by the deference that many courts give to national security. Local police, while sometimes not forthcoming about what they are doing, are not shielded by secrecy laws. Groups such as the American Civil Liberties Union and local police review boards may find it easier to mount legal challenges. Further, what courts decide in local cases may eventually create new principles or precedents that bear on larger national issues.

Chapter 4

Online Privacy and Schools

In November 2009 fifteen-year-old Harrington High School student Blake Robbins was hauled into the principal's office and told he would be disciplined for improper behavior—for something he had allegedly done at home. Blake and other students at high schools in the Lower Merion School District in Pennsylvania then discovered that a secret program had been installed on their school-issued laptops, as part of a $720,000 security and antitheft program. The program could be used not only to track the device's location but also to surreptitiously take pictures through its webcam. The pictures had shown Robbins in his bedroom swallowing what the school officials claimed to be illegal pills. (Robbins's parents and their attorney said they were actually Mike and Ike candies.)

Although the program was supposed to be used only to trace stolen computers, the district's attorney admitted in court that at least fifty-six thousand webcam images had been captured and stored on the district's server. Robbins alone had been photographed more than four hundred times, often when he was asleep or half undressed. The program also took screen shots of instant messages or video chats between Robbins and his friends.

In October 2010 the school district agreed to pay $610,000 to settle the suits by Robbins and two other students. Meanwhile, the FBI, the US attorney, and the local district attorney jointly investigated the school district but eventually decided that there was no evidence of criminal intent on the part of school officials. A Senate hearing led to proposed legislation that would prohibit such surveillance programs in the future.

Surveillance for Safety?

Although the Robbins case is an extreme example in that it reached beyond the school into students' homes, in recent years the surveillance and tracking of students in high schools and even middle schools has become widespread and extensive. Today's students are tracked throughout the school day, during every class or activity anywhere on the campus. This tracking is enabled by cameras as well as school-issued ID cards that contain chips that can be read by scanners placed throughout the school.

The main reason given for expanding school surveillance is ensuring the safety of students and faculty. High-profile school shootings such as those at Columbine High School in Colorado (where two students killed thirteen people in 1999) and at Sandy Hook Elementary School in Connecticut (where one young man fatally shot twenty children and six adult staff members in 2012) have made schools appear to be unsafe environments. The odds of becoming a victim of a school shooting are vanishingly small. A more prevalent threat is that of drugs, drug-related crimes, and gang activity. On top of this, after 9/11 the federal government also decided that schools might be terrorist targets. The government made matching funds available for schools to install elaborate new surveillance systems.

> "Schools are one of the key social settings where innovations in surveillance technology are first deployed."[38]
>
> —*John Gilliom and Torin Monahan, writers on surveillance issues.*

There is broad support for programs that are seen to be necessary safety measures. Parents, after all, have many valid concerns about their children's safety in a world where it is hard to protect them from criminals and dangerous temptations such as drugs. Children spend a large portion of their waking hours in school, and schools in a way must act as a kind of surrogate parent. This certainly includes a duty to provide protection.

On the other hand, while students' privacy rights are limited compared to those of adults, there is concern that overprotective, overly intrusive measures may have the effect of training young people to accept a society in which their privacy as adults will be similarly compromised. There is also a concern that technologies first applied to

Mourners visit a memorial for the victims of the Sandy Hook Elementary School shooting in 2012. Surveillance at schools across the country has increased in the wake of high-profile shootings.

students may later be used with adult citizens. As two writers on surveillance issues note: "Schools are one of the key social settings where innovations in surveillance technology are first deployed. In a pattern similar to what we see in prisons and the military, the availability of large numbers of semi-citizens under daily institutional control has made schools leading laboratories for new surveillance practices."[38]

Responding to Cyberbullying

Another issue that has led to a clash between student privacy and the need for protection involves cyberbullying, or the use of online communications or social networks by one student (or group of students) to harass, ridicule, or intimidate another. In February 2010 Megan Wisemore, a freshman at Oak Grove High School in Missouri, posted a Facebook message warning her friends that another student was a "skank" and saying that she hated the other girl. Although the message was only intended for her friends, the other student eventually

The Human Solution?

Perhaps one way to reduce schools' intrusion into students' online privacy is to provide alternative ways to fight online bullying or threats. Instead of relying on problematic technology or inflexible rules, one writer suggests that students and administrators should focus on developing a relationship of trust:

> Schools should work to develop a culture where everyone looks out for everyone else and if something of concern arises someone will step up and take appropriate action. Most of the time, when there is a threat to cause harm—either to one's self or others—someone sees or hears about it. What do they do at that moment? Are they empowered to take action themselves? Do students feel comfortable talking with an adult at school about what they witnessed or heard about? Do they feel that telling an adult at school or at home would resolve the situation?

Justin W. Patchin, "Should Schools Monitor Students' Social Media Accounts?," Cyberbullying Research Center, September 17, 2013. http://cyberbullying.us.

saw the message and physically attacked Megan. Both students received suspensions. Megan's mother objected: "It was very colorful language that I don't approve of, but I didn't like the fact the school stepped into my home. That's her constitutional right to speak what she feels."[39]

Sometimes the consequences of cyberbullying can be much worse. On September 9, 2013, in Polk County, Florida, twelve-year-old Rebecca Sedwick jumped to her death after other teenagers sent her repeated electronic messages with "drink bleach and die"[40] and similar taunts. According to the county sheriff who arrested two girls for stalking Sedwick, as many as fifteen teenagers may have participated in the online harassment. The charges were later dropped, but Sedwick's mother is considering filing a wrongful death suit.

Because of the potential consequences, school officials must try to detect and prevent cyberbullying. In the Oak Grove case, school officials said they were simply reacting to a troublesome situation that had come to their attention. However, important privacy issues can arise when schools monitor social media and other online activity to watch for signs of cyberbullying, drugs or gangs, or even students who might be suffering from serious psychological problems.

Drawing the Line

In 2012 at Griffith Middle School in Indiana, three eighth-grade students were expelled for Facebook postings in which, according to a legal complaint filed on behalf of the students, "the conversation spanned numerous subjects, from the pain of cutting oneself while shaving to the girl's friendship, before turning to a discussion of which classmates they'd like to kill if they had the chance. At all times, the conversation was purely in jest . . . as is evidenced by the girl's repeated use of 'emoticons' . . . [and] abbreviations (like lol) and consistent capitalization intended to represent sarcasm."[41] Despite this context and the fact the students were posting from home on their own computers, the school expelled them for violating its rules against bullying, intimidation, and harassment. This raises a number of concerns. A basic problem is whether the adults who are trying to assess the students' postings really understand them. They would have to be familiar not only

"It was very colorful language that I don't approve of, but I didn't like the fact the school stepped into my home. That's her constitutional right to speak what she feels."[39]

—*The mother of an expelled student.*

with ever-changing teenage slang but also understand the abbreviations and emoticons used commonly online. This is particularly important because these often cryptic phrases are the only way nuances such as humor or sarcasm can be communicated online, where voice tone and body language are not available. It can be very hard to tell whether a statement is an actual threat of violence that must be taken seriously. This difficulty in reacting appropriately to students' online activities may be compounded if a school uses zero-tolerance rules where any identified behavior automatically triggers suspension or expulsion, leaving no room for judgment based on the particular circumstances. No school official wants to miss what might turn out to be the early signs of a threat of violence or suicide. On the other hand, if students believe that what they say online is not only being continually monitored, but may result in harsh, possibly arbitrary action, this may make it hard to learn how to balance freedom of expression and responsibility for one's words.

The courts have been struggling to determine the appropriate boundaries for students' use of social media. A broad principle was worked out in a free speech case in 1969, during a period when a growing number of students were engaging in political protests. That year the Supreme Court declared that school officials could not restrict speech, or symbolic acts, such as wearing an armband to protest the Vietnam War, unless they "materially and substantially interfere with the requirements of appropriate discipline in the operation of the school."[42]

Today, however, with students spending hours each day using Facebook, Twitter, and other social media, school walls seem no longer to be a meaningful boundary. In the Oak Grove case, words posted at home led to a fight on campus. Provocative speech could create a situation that would make appropriate discipline at school difficult to maintain.

In a 2010 case (*Layshock v. Hermitage School District*), the court ruled that a student whose posting described the principal as a "big whore"[43] should not have been suspended from school. However, in another case in the same court circuit (*J.S. v. Blue Mountain School District*), the judge upheld the suspension of a student whose posting had called the principal a "tight ass" who liked "hitting on students and parents."[44] In the latter case, the judges apparently decided that the speech was provocative enough that it could cause substantial disruption in school. These different outcomes suggest how hazy the line between acceptable and unacceptable student postings might be.

Justin Silverman of the Digital Media Law Project believes that courts should move in the direction of protecting rather than restricting student speech online. He points out that "Wisemore didn't interfere with her school when she posted to Facebook. Wisemore's classmate brought that speech into the classroom and caused a disturbance by starting a fight. That classmate should be the only student suspended."[45] As for the students who insulted principals online, Silverman suggests:

> The comments made by [these two students] didn't interfere with the schooling of any students. They targeted principals, and as offensive as their comments may be, those students shouldn't be punished unless that speech enters the classroom and causes a disturbance. For those who are the subject of on-line rants, there are legal remedies available when the speech is actionable, such as laws against libel and harassment.[46]

Monitoring Online Activity

Schools may be held legally liable if they know about a developing situation (such as a threat by one student against other students) and do not intervene. Concerns about legal liability, as well as a desire to

Pallbearers wearing antibullying T-shirts carry the casket of Rebecca Sedwick, a twelve-year-old girl who jumped to her death in 2013 after repeated online taunting. Cyberbullying has forced school officials nationwide to seek a balance between student privacy and safety.

Teaching Students to Protect Themselves Online

The Children's Internet Protection Act of 2000 essentially required public schools to install Internet-filtering software to block websites or communications that have objectionable content related to violence, drug use, or sex. Often social networking sites are blocked as well. Additionally, monitoring software can be used to record students' searches and online communications, activities that they may feel to be sensitive and private.

The effectiveness of blocking or monitoring is limited, however, since tech-savvy students can get around it, and many students now have smartphones or other devices—which some schools have tried to ban or restrict as well. Even if a safe, sanitized sector of cyberspace could be created for students, this may not necessarily be a good idea. Jim Bosco and Keith Krueger of the Consortium for School Networking warn, "Highly restrictive Internet and mobile policies in the school environment provide only a false sense of protecting kids."

The American Library Association believes that simply blocking social media "does not teach safe behavior and leaves youth without the necessary knowledge and skills to protect their privacy or engage in responsible speech." Rather, librarians and teachers are urged to "educate minors to participate responsibly, ethically, and safely."

Quoted in Laura Varlas, "Can Social Media and School Policies Be 'Friends'?," *Policy Priorities*, Winter 2011. www.ascd.org.

prevent tragic consequences, are leading some schools to use software or services to monitor students' online activity and trigger alerts if harmful speech or activity is detected.

In September 2013 the Glendale, California, school district paid $40,500 to Geo Listening, a firm that specializes in monitoring social media. The contract called for the accounts of fourteen thousand middle and high school students on Facebook, Twitter, and other social media to be monitored for a year for indications that students may be victims or perpetrators of cyberbullying or other problem behaviors. Richard Sheehan, the superintendent of the Glendale school district, said the necessity for the surveillance program was shown by the suicides of two students in the past two years. He noted that funds for person-to-person mental health services had been cut and hoped that technology could help fill the gap. Sheehan noted that thanks to a pilot project the previous spring, a potential suicide had already been prevented. Another student was questioned (but not disciplined) after he posted what turned out to be a picture of a fake gun. In appropriate cases, such as the threat of a school shooting, police would be called.

The scope of what is being monitored raises questions, however. Geo Listening also reports when students are talking about drug use or cutting class. Even the amount of time students spend using their smartphone in class is noted. Lee Tien, senior staff attorney for the Electronic Frontier Foundation, an online rights advocacy group, suggests that schools are going too far in their quest for security: "This is the government essentially hiring a contractor to stalk the social media of the kids. When the government—and public schools are part of the government—engages in any kind of line-crossing and to actually go and gather information about people away from school, that crosses a line."[47]

> "When the government—and public schools are part of the government—engages in any kind of line-crossing and to actually go and gather information about people away from school, that crosses a line."[47]
>
> —Lee Tien, senior staff attorney for the Electronic Frontier Foundation.

Protecting Student Information

Some schools have started to use online services with software designed to, for example, automatically assess students' work or monitor their completion of homework. But although this software (now an estimated $8 billion industry) may improve student performance and graduation rates, the relative lack of security may raise new privacy issues, according to a study by Fordham University law professor Joel R. Reidenberg. He says, "We found that when school districts are transferring student information to cloud service providers, by and large key privacy protections are absent from those arrangements, We're worried about the implications for students over time, how their personal information may be used or misused."[48]

Reidenberg found that few of the contracts involving this software specified what student information might be disclosed and for what purposes or that data would not be sold or used for marketing purposes. Parents were usually not informed about how student data might be used. In part, this situation seems to mirror the general lack of clear, understandable privacy policies throughout the online world.

Schools of the twenty-first century are called on to raise educational standards to enable students to compete in a rapidly changing world. At the same time, they are charged with protecting students from outsiders and from one another. In an online world that effectively has no boundaries—no inside or outside—the privacy rights of students, like those of adult citizens, are undergoing a messy process of negotiation.

Chapter 5

Balancing Privacy and Security

Although the objectives (stopping terrorism, fighting crime, or protecting students) may be different, the tools used by the government to obtain and analyze people's communications and personal data are similar. This means the same issues tend to crop up everywhere from the White House to the local police station or public school. Context does matter, however. Measures that might be reluctantly accepted if they prevent another 9/11 attack might be prudently rejected if offered as a solution to vandalism or teenage mischief.

Broadly speaking, the government and its supporters argue that these tools are necessary to provide the security people need and deserve in an increasingly dangerous world. Privacy is just part of the equation, and one must trust the democratic process to come up with leaders who will act responsibly even though security requires secrecy. But given a history of out-of-control secret programs in the 1970s and in the first years of this century, how realistic is this hope?

On the other hand, privacy advocates focus on identifying abuses and proposing strict laws to protect the rights of citizens. But how can one have both strict oversight and enough flexibility for the agencies charged with protecting security to do their job? Many potential vulnerabilities exist in the online world, and only increasingly sophisticated software may be able to keep up with the threat in real time.

Checks and Balances

Whatever view or values one holds, one must work within the existing political system. One of the first things taught about government in civics class is that it has three distinct branches: the executive, the legislative, and the judicial. The US Constitution provides for a system of checks and balances in which each branch has enough power to carry out its own functions, while preventing any one branch from becoming too powerful.

Where privacy issues are concerned, however, this system may not function well. The executive branch under the president has the primary responsibility for security. Upon taking office, each new president is briefed by security agencies about potential threats and the necessity of surveillance and data-gathering programs for keeping up with an ever-changing threat. Since much of this information is classified, it is hard for the president to receive opposing views. Further, just as no president during the Cold War wanted to be seen as being "soft on communism," none wants to be seen as soft on terrorism, or worse, having failed to stop a major attack.

The legislature (Congress) is supposed to create the legal framework that the executive branch uses to carry out its objectives. However, members of Congress face many of the same difficulties as the president. Some may receive secret briefings. In general, the details of data-gathering programs are mysterious and technical. And at least until recently, privacy issues were not among the top concerns of voters anyway.

> "[Courts] must abandon the task of identifying difficult-to-identify expectations of privacy . . . and instead return to the task of preserving the environment that makes privacy possible."[49]
>
> —Marc Jonathan Bliz, legal scholar.

The judicial branch is supposed to be the final bulwark against abuses and the upholder of the Constitution. However, judges share many of the same problems as executives or legislators. Evidence may be secret as well as being hard to evaluate. The claim of state secrecy is often given great deference. How should the courts deal with their task? Can narrowly defined legal requirements keep up with rapidly changing technology? According to one legal scholar, courts "must abandon the task of identifying difficult-to-identify expectations of privacy . . . and instead return to the task of preserving the environment that makes privacy possible."[49]

A review panel established by President Barack Obama (pictured in 2013) made various recommendations to address concerns about government surveillance. Some members of Congress believe the review panel went too far, while others say it did not go far enough.

In December 2013 one federal court took the narrow approach, relying on the precedent in *Smith v. Maryland* that people do not have an expectation of privacy for their phone number or related information. Another court, however, said that the mass collection of such data was likely to be unconstitutional. Does a practice that might be innocuous when applied to just a few people become problematic when records are scooped up by the millions?

Often if an issue is important enough and lower courts disagree, the Supreme Court eventually decides the case. For many of the key conflicts between government objectives and privacy rights, however, this has not yet happened.

Reform Proposals

Meanwhile, in the wake of Edward Snowden's revelations, in December 2013 the President's Review Group on Intelligence and

Communications Technologies made a number of recommendations to address concerns about the recently revealed surveillance programs. Among them were the following:

> We recommend that Congress should end such storage [of metadata] and transition to a system in which such metadata is held privately for the government to query when necessary for national security purposes.

> With respect to the FISC [US Foreign Intelligence Surveillance Court], we recommend that Congress should create the position of Public Interest Advocate to represent the interests of privacy and civil liberties before the FISC.

> The US Government should take additional steps to promote security, by (1) fully supporting and not undermining efforts to create encryption standards; (2) making clear that it will not in any way subvert, undermine, weaken, or make vulnerable generally available commercial encryption.[50]

"Without further reforms, the American people still won't get the information they need to make up their own minds about these programs."[51]

—Senator Al Franken.

Some members of Congress believe that neither Obama nor his review panel go far enough in addressing surveillance issues, but others believe they have gone too far. In 2013 Senator Al Franken introduced the Surveillance Transparency Act, which would require the government to report annually in some detail on its surveillance practices. Franken insists, "Without further reforms, the American people still won't get the information they need to make up their own minds about these programs. Seven months after the Snowden leaks, the American government has yet to tell the American people how many of them were caught up in this surveillance—and how many actually had their information looked at."[51] On the other side of the debate, Represen-

1984 Versus 2014

The ultimate fictional depiction of the final death of privacy is George Orwell's novel *Nineteen Eighty-Four*, published in 1949. In the book, Orwell's writes,

> There was of course no way of knowing whether you were being watched at any given moment. How often, or on what system, the Thought Police plugged in on any individual wire was guesswork. It was even conceivable that they watched everybody all the time. But at any rate they could plug in your wire whenever they wanted to. You had to live—did live, from habit that became instinct—in the assumption that every sound you made was overheard, and, except in darkness, every movement scrutinized.

Orwell was writing just after a war that featured a clash between two totalitarian systems—Hitler's Germany and Stalin's Russia. Orwell imagined how such systems would use television and other new electronic technologies of the time. The adjective *Orwellian* is still used today to describe the way absolute power destroys privacy and even language itself.

The year 2014 is rather different from the fictional year 1984 in a number of ways, however. There is no single Thought Police, but rather networks of agencies that have various objectives. Instead of one screen to deliver propaganda while spying on the viewer, there are many screens, and the flow of information goes both ways. Modern digital technology can empower governments but also give ordinary citizens tools to record events, communicate in real time, and organize social movements.

George Orwell, *Nineteen Eighty-Four*. New York: Harcourt, Brace, 1949.

tative Michele Bachmann opposed further disclosure of surveillance details, which "could mean giving an extra level of protection to suspected terrorists that goes above and beyond the rights of the American people."[52]

Privacy in 2025

In 2014, on the twenty-fifth anniversary of the development of the World Wide Web, the Pew Research Center published a report that examined what the web might look like in ten years. Among the suggestions of experts cited in the report, the following seem most relevant to the fate of privacy:

- A global, immersive, invisible, ambient networked computing environment built through the continued proliferation of smart sensors, cameras, software, databases, and massive data centers in a world-spanning information fabric known as the Internet of Things. . . .
- Tagging, databasing, and intelligent analytical mapping of the physical and social realms. . . .
- The Internet of Things, artificial intelligence, and big data will make people more aware of their world and their own behavior. . . .
- Political awareness and action will be facilitated and more peaceful change *and* public uprisings like the Arab Spring will emerge. . . .
- Abuses and abusers will "evolve and scale." Human nature isn't changing; there's laziness, bullying, stalking, stupidity, pornography, dirty tricks, crime, and those who practice them have new capacity to make life miserable for others. . . .
- Pressured by these changes, governments and corporations will try to assert power—and at times succeed—as they invoke security and cultural norms. . . .
- People will continue—sometimes grudgingly—to make tradeoffs favoring convenience and perceived immediate gains over privacy; and privacy will be something only the upscale will enjoy. . . .
- Foresight and accurate predictions can make a difference; "The best way to predict the future is to invent it."

Janna Anderson and Lee Rainie, "Digital Life in 2025," Pew Research Internet Project, March 11, 2014. www.pewinternet.org.

Protecting the Innocent

Even as the controversy builds over what information should be gathered and what people should be told about the process, some agreement might be possible in cases where innocent people are harmed. Daniel J. Steinbock suggests that creating mechanisms for more oversight and independent review of how data is obtained and used may be helpful in preventing abuses even if it complicates security efforts.

Steinbock suggests several steps that could be taken to provide due process and to minimize the harm caused by mistaken or misleading information. First, he says, the government should provide a simple way that a person can immediately challenge and try to reverse "denial of access to flights or infringements of other liberty or property rights." He adds that affected persons should also have the right to "examine the information being used and have it corrected in the database(s)."[53] If it is found that the faulty information has caused financial harm (such as an airline ticket that could not be used and cannot be refunded), the individual could be given monetary compensation.

Steinbock's final suggestion goes beyond trying to make things right for the victims of secret information-gathering programs. He proposes that the computer algorithms used to match people to profiles be examined by "independent oversight bodies"[54] that can determine the accuracy of the system and the procedures for dealing with errors.

What Individuals Can Do

Individuals can also reduce the possible impact of government privacy abuses. Information cannot be abused by either government or private individuals if that information is not online in the first place. Thus, carefully considering what should be posted on social network sites or sent via e-mail or other forms of electronic communication is always advisable. The biggest sifter and miner of the information people put online is not the government but the companies that provide the online entertainment, services, and applications that so many people enjoy today. The same information that is used to show advertising, make recommendations, or create customer profiles is also available to governments, either through legal process or mass data gathering.

There are also the options of encryption and anonymity. In response to the revelations of government surveillance, companies such as Google have said they are strengthening the encryption of data passing through their servers. Individuals can also obtain software to encrypt the contents of their hard drives. The encryption and other security of popular cloud data-storage services can also be investigated. There are also services such as Tor that remove much of the identifying information attached to web searches and other online transactions—but none of these methods is perfect. Unless one goes off the grid and lives a hermit-like existence, there are limits to what an individual can do to preserve privacy.

> "Privacy has a social value. When the law protects the individual, it does so not just for the individual's sake but for the sake of society."[56]
>
> —*Law professor Daniel J. Solove.*

Reframing the Issue

Perhaps, though, posing each issue as privacy versus security may be the wrong way to look at things. Daniel J. Solove suggests:

> The argument that privacy and security are mutually exclusive stems from what I call the "all-or-nothing fallacy." Sacrificing privacy doesn't automatically make us more secure. Not all security measures are invasive of privacy. Moreover, no correlation has been established between the effectiveness of a security measure and a corresponding decrease in liberty. In other words, the most effective security measures need not be the most detrimental to liberty.[55]

Solove is essentially asking policy makers and citizens to take a more thoughtful approach before considering new programs that could impact privacy. Policy makers could ask whether there is actual evidence that, for example, scooping up everyone's phone calls can provide relevant information in time to prevent a terrorist attack. Perhaps better training of agents on the ground and promoting better relationships with local communities might be a wiser investment for some of the resources being spent on mass surveillance programs.

Further, Solove argues that "privacy has a social value. When the law protects the individual, it does so not just for the individual's sake but for the sake of society. Privacy thus shouldn't be weighed as an individual right against the greater social good. Privacy issues involve balancing societal interests on both sides of the scale."[56]

These views suggest that a proposed surveillance program should be looked at using a broad definition of *security* that includes the effects of the surveillance on people's confidence in online services and the ability of people and companies to carry on their lawful business online. One should also consider the possible effects the atmosphere created by surveillance has on society and the global Internet itself. The question then becomes, how can privacy *and* security both be enhanced?

Companies that provide online entertainment services collect far more information about consumers than the government. To protect privacy, consumers need to be mindful of the information they provide to these and other online businesses.

The Many Possible Futures of Privacy

Futurists looking at the ultimate fate of privacy come to differing conclusions. If present trends continue with only minor adjustments here and there, *New York Times* columnist Ross Douthat thinks the future might be one in which privacy continues to gradually diminish while most people come to accept the lack of privacy as the normal. He writes:

> Our government will enjoy extraordinary, potentially tyrannical powers, but most citizens will be monitored without feeling persecuted or coerced.
>
> So instead of a climate of pervasive fear, there will be a chilling effect at the margins of political discourse, mostly affecting groups and opinions considered disreputable already. Instead of a top-down program of political repression, there will be a more haphazard pattern of politically motivated, Big Data–enabled abuses. . . .
>
> In this atmosphere, radicalism and protest will seem riskier, paranoia will be more reasonable, and conspiracy theories will proliferate. But because genuinely dangerous people will often be pre-empted or more swiftly caught, the privacy-for-security swap will seem like a reasonable trade-off to many Americans—especially when there is no obvious alternative short of disconnecting from the Internet entirely.[57]

Back at the turn of this century, science-fiction writer and futurist David Brin offered a more radical and provocative point of view. He believes that society must find a way to live in a world in which most things will *not* be private. This is in part because the technology that is so convenient and empowering depends for its operation on the free exchange of information about people's desires and preferences. For Brin, the ultimate focus should not be on privacy, but transparency—the ability of citizens to know what their government is doing and thus be able to hold it accountable. Says Brin:

Privacy is a highly desirable *product* of liberty. If we remain free and sovereign, then we'll have a little privacy—in our bedrooms and sanctuaries. As citizens, we'll be able to demand some.

But *accountability* is no side benefit. It is the one fundamental ingredient on which liberty thrives. Without the accountability that derives from openness—enforceable upon even the mightiest individuals and institutions—freedom must surely die. . . .

One of the basic decisions we all face in times ahead will be this:

Can we stand living our lives exposed to scrutiny . . . our secrets laid out in the open . . . if in return we get flashlights of our own, that we can shine on the arrogant and strong?

Or is privacy's illusion so precious that it is worth any price, including surrendering our own right to pierce the schemes of the powerful?[58]

Shaping the Future

Will Douthat's, Brin's, or another future prevail? As young people of the digital generation increasingly move into positions of greater responsibility and decision-making ability, they will have to shape the policies and rules that will determine what privacy means later in the century. Speaking before the 2014 South by Southwest Interactive Conference, law professor Robert Chesney notes, "It was in vogue for a while for people to say that the up-and-coming generation doesn't care about privacy. . . . It's clear now that was at best overstated, and probably reflected a failure to appreciate the real implications of what moving to a world of digitized information means."[59]

> "Can we stand living our lives exposed to scrutiny . . . our secrets laid out in the open . . . if in return we get flashlights of our own, that we can shine on the arrogant and strong?"[58]
>
> —*Futurist David Brin.*

What can people who care about privacy do? Consider the implications of emerging technology for both security and privacy. Think about what information one is exposing online and in the activities of daily life. Participate in the democratic process so that legislators and government officials are aware of the need for a more robust debate and greater institutional accountability. In the long run, this is the best way to ensure a sensible balance between privacy, transparency, and security.

Source Notes

Introduction: A Shifting Balance

1. Quoted in Glenn Greenwald, "Edward Snowden: The Whistle-blower Behind the NSA Surveillance Revelations," *Guardian* (London), June 9, 2013. www.theguardian.com.
2. Barack Obama, "Remarks by the President on Review of Signals Intelligence," White House, January 17, 2014. www.whitehouse.gov.
3. Obama, "Remarks by the President on Review of Signals Intelligence."

Chapter 1: Privacy and the Challenge of Technology

4. Quoted in Philippa Strum, *Privacy: The Debate in the United States Since 1945*. Fort Worth, TX: Harcourt, 1998, p. 116.
5. *Boyd v. United States*, 116 US 616 (1886).
6. *Brinegar v. United States*, 338 US 160 (1949).
7. Samuel D. Warren and Louis Brandeis, "The Right to Privacy," *Harvard Law Review*, vol. 4, no. 5, December 15, 1890, p. 193.
8. *Olmstead v. United States*, 277 US 438 (1928).
9. *Olmstead v. United States*.
10. *Katz v. United States*, 389 US 347 (1967).
11. *Katz v. United States*.
12. Susan W. Brenner and Leo L. Clarke, "Fourth Amendment Protection for Shared Privacy Rights in Stored Transactional Data," *Brooklyn Journal of Law and Policy*, vol. 14, no. 1, November 14, 2005, p. 31.
13. Select Committee to Study Governmental Operations with Respect to Intelligence Activities, *Intelligence Activities and the Rights of Americans*, book 2, US Senate. Washington, DC: US Government Printing Office, 1976. www.intelligence.senate.gov.

14. Select Committee to Study Governmental Operations with Respect to Intelligence Activities, *Intelligence Activities and the Rights of Americans.*
15. Marc Rotenberg, "Privacy and Secrecy After September 11," *Minnesota Law Review*, vol. 86, no. 6, 2002.
16. Report of the Secretary's Advisory Committee on Automated Personal Data Systems, *Records, Computers, and the Rights of Citizens.* Washington, DC: US Department of Health, Education, and Welfare, 1973, p. viii.

Chapter 2: Online Privacy and the War on Terrorism

17. In re Motion for Release of Court Records, 526 F. Supp. 2d 484 (FISA Ct. Rev. 2007).
18. Quoted in *USA Today*, "Pentagon's 'Terror Information Awareness' Program Will End," September 25, 2003. http://usatoday30 .usatoday.com.
19. James Bamford, "The NSA Is Building the Country's Biggest Spy Center (Watch What You Say)," *Wired*, March 15, 2012. www .wired.com.
20. Quoted in Steven Levy, "How the NSA Almost Killed the Internet—and Why It Still Could," *Wired*, February 7, 2014. www .wired.com/2014/01/how-the-us-almost-killed-the-internet.
21. Quoted in Levy, "How the NSA Almost Killed the Internet."
22. Quoted in Levy, "How the NSA Almost Killed the Internet."
23. Quoted in Levy, "How the NSA Almost Killed the Internet."
24. Quoted in Levy, "How the NSA Almost Killed the Internet."
25. New America Foundation, "Do NSA's Bulk Surveillance Programs Stop Terrorists?," January 13, 2014. www.newamerica.net.
26. Daniel J. Solove, "Reconstructing Electronic Surveillance Law," *George Washington Law Review*, vol. 72, 2004. http://papers.ssrn .com.
27. Daniel J. Solove, *The Digital Person: Technology and Privacy in the Information Age.* New York: New York University Press, 2004, p. 181.
28. Daniel J. Steinbock, "Data Matching, Data Mining, and Due Process," *Georgia Law Review*, vol. 40, no. 1, 2005, pp. 82–83.

29. Whitfield Diffie and Susan Landau, *Privacy on the Line*, 2nd ed. Cambridge, MA: MIT Press, 2007, p. 328.

30. Nicole Perlroth, Jeff Larson, and Scott Shane, "N.S.A. Able to Foil Basic Safeguards of Security on Web," *New York Times*, September 5, 2013. www.nytimes.com.

31. Quinn Norton, "Byte Rights: War Is Peace, Vulns Are National Security," *Maximum PC*, March 2014, p. 12.

Chapter 3: Online Privacy and Law Enforcement

32. Quoted in Al Baker, "In Pursuit of Killer, Police Mine Online Clues," *New York Times*, May 2, 2011, p. A20.

33. *New York Times*, "Twitter Tapping," editorial, December 13, 2009. www.nytimes.com.

34. Michael D. Silva, "Undercover Online: Why Your Agency Needs a Social Network Investigations Policy," *Police Chief*, March 2014. www.policechiefmagazine.org.

35. Testimony of Mark Marshall in "Going Dark: Lawful Electronic Surveillance in the Face of New Technologies," hearing before the Subcommittee on Crime, Terrorism, and Homeland Security of the Committee on the Judiciary, House of Representatives, February 17, 2011. www.gpo.gov.

36. *United States v. Jones*, 565 US ___ (2012).

37. Quoted in Somini Sengupta, "Privacy Fears as Surveillance Grows in Cities," *New York Times*, October 14, 2013, p. 1.

Chapter 4: Online Privacy and Schools

38. John Gilliom and Torin Monahan, *SuperVision: An Introduction to the Surveillance Society*. Chicago: University of Chicago Press, 2012.

39. Quoted in Justin Silverman, "Keeping Online Speech Outside the Schoolhouse Gate," *Justin Silverman's blog*, Digital Media Law Project, March 17, 2010. www.dmlp.org.

40. Mike Schneider, "Bullying Charges Dropped Against Girls in Rebecca Sedwick Suicide Case," *Huffpost Miami*, November 21, 2013. www.huffingtonpost.com.

41. Quoted in legal complaint filed in U.S. District Court, Northern District of Indiana, Hammond Division, April 24, 2012. www.splc.org/pdf/sm_complaint.pdf.

42. *Tinker v. Des Moines Independent Community School District*, 393 US 503 (1969).

43. *Layshock v. Hermitage School District*, No. 07-4465 (US 3rd Circuit Court of Appeals, 2011).

44. *J.S. v. Blue Mountain School District*, No. 08-4138 (US 3rd Circuit Court of Appeals, 2011).

45. Silverman, "Keeping Online Speech Outside the Schoolhouse Gate."

46. Silverman, "Keeping Online Speech Outside the Schoolhouse Gate."

47. Quoted in Michael Martinez, "California School District Hires Firm to Monitor Students' Social Media," CNN, September 18, 2013. www.cnn.com.

48. Quoted in Natasha Singer, "Schools Use Web Tools, and Data Is Seen at Risk," *New York Times*, December 13, 2013, p. A26.

Chapter 5: Balancing Privacy and Security

49. Marc Jonathan Bliz, "Video Surveillance and the Constitution of Public Space: Fitting the Fourth Amendment to a World That Tracks Image and Identity," *University of Texas Law Review*, vol. 82, no. 6, May 2004, p. 1481.

50. President's Review Group on Intelligence and Communications Technologies, *Liberty and Security in a Changing World*, December 12, 2013. www.whitehouse.gov.

51. Quoted in Devin Henry, "Members of Congress Still Want Their Shot at Surveillance Reform," *MinnPost*, January 17, 2014. www.minnpost.com.

52. Quoted in Henry, "Members of Congress Still Want Their Shot at Surveillance Reform."

53. Steinbock, "Data Matching, Data Mining, and Due Process," p. 85.

54. Steinbock, "Data Matching, Data Mining, and Due Process," p. 85.

55. Daniel J. Solove, *Nothing to Hide: The False Tradeoff Between Privacy and Security*. New Haven, CT: Yale University Press, 2011, p. 33.
56. Solove, *Nothing to Hide*, p. 201.
57. Ross Douthat, "Your Smartphone Is Watching You," *New York Times*, June 9, 2013, p. 11.
58. David Brin, "The Transparent Society," *Wired*. www.wired.com.
59. Quoted in Adam Satariano and Alex Barinka, "Over-Sharing Crowd to Ponder Privacy at SXSW," *Bloomberg*, March 7, 2014. www.bloomberg.com.

Online Privacy Tips

Basic Security

- Use security software to block viruses and malware. Keep it up to date.
- Use passwords at least eight characters long. Add numerals and punctuation to make them harder to guess.
- Back up important data to a flash or USB drive or an online service.

E-mail and Messaging

- Do not click on web links or attachments in e-mail or text messages unless you are expecting them. (Strange messages from a friend may indicate that their account has been "hijacked.")
- Beware of "scary" messages that claim to be from a bank or government agency. Contact the agency directly if you think there might be a problem.
- Do not put credit card numbers or other sensitive information in e-mail or text messages.

Web and Social Networks

- Learn about browser features that can enhance security and privacy.
- Find and use the privacy settings for Facebook, Twitter, and other social networks.
- Do not post personal details or other information that you wouldn't want a stranger to know.

Banking and E-Commerce

- Make payments only on secure web pages (indicated by https:// in the address and a padlock symbol).

- Do not do banking or online purchases on a public Wifi network.
- Monitor bank and credit card accounts regularly for signs of fraud.

Mobile Devices

- Protect your phone or tablet with a passcode.
- Install software that allows you to track or disable lost or stolen devices.
- Install apps from only trusted sources.
- Check settings to see what information apps may be obtaining from your device.

Finally . . .

- Think before you hit "Send." You cannot take your words back.
- Common sense and courtesy can go a long way.

Related Organizations and Websites

American Civil Liberties Union (ACLU)

125 Broad St., 18th Floor
New York, NY 10004
(212) 549-2500
www.aclu.org

The ACLU is a nonprofit organization that advocates and litigates for constitutional rights, including privacy, equal protection, due process, and freedom of speech.

Center for Democracy and Technology

1634 I St. NW, #1100
Washington, DC 20006
(202) 637-9800
www.cdt.org

The Center for Democracy and Technology is a research and advocacy group that specializes in issues raised by technology, including surveillance and privacy.

Electronic Frontier Foundation

815 Eddy St.
San Francisco, CA 94109
(415) 436-9333
www.eff.org

The Electronic Frontier Foundation was one of the first and most comprehensive organizations devoted to legal action and activism for privacy and consumer rights.

Electronic Privacy Information Center (EPIC)

1718 Connecticut Ave. NW, Suite 200
Washington, DC 20009
(202) 483-1140
www.epic.org

EPIC is a public interest research organization that focuses on privacy and free speech rights in connection with new and emerging technologies.

Federal Bureau of Investigation (FBI)

935 Pennsylvania Ave. NW
Washington, DC 20535-0001
(202) 324-3000
www.fbi.gov

The FBI investigates federal crime (including cybercrime) and performs counterintelligence and antiterrorist activities.

National Security Agency

(301) 688-6524
www.nsa.gov

The National Security Agency specializes in signals intelligence and surveillance, cryptography, and cybersecurity.

US Department of Homeland Security (DHS)

245 Murray Ln. SW
Washington, DC 20528-0075
(202) 282-8000
www.dhs.gov

The DHS is a consolidated federal agency responsible for border security, cybersecurity, fighting terrorism, and responding to attacks and natural disasters.

For Further Research

Books

Julia Angwin, *Dragnet Nation: A Quest for Privacy, Security, and Freedom in a World of Relentless Surveillance*. New York: Times Books, 2014.

Whitfield Diffie and Susan Landau, *Privacy on the Line: The Politics of Wiretapping and Encryption*. 2nd ed. Cambridge, MA: MIT Press, 2010.

Sylvia Engdahl, ed., *Domestic Wiretapping*. Detroit, MI: Greenhaven, 2008.

John Gilliom and Torin Monahan, *SuperVision: An Introduction to the Surveillance Society*. Chicago: University of Chicago Press, 2013.

David Houle, *Is Privacy Dead? The Future of Privacy in the Digital Age*. Houle, 2013. Kindle edition.

Noel Merino, ed., *Teens and Privacy*. Detroit, MI: Greenhaven, 2011.

Daniel J. Solove, *Nothing to Hide: The False Tradeoff Between Privacy and Security*. New Haven, CT: Yale University Press, 2011.

Websites

Cory Doctorow (blog), *Guardian* (www.theguardian.com/profile /corydoctorow). The blog of a science-fiction writer and prominent privacy and Internet freedom advocate, with many posts related to privacy issues.

Online Guide to Privacy Resources (www.epic.org/privacy/privacy _resources_faq.html). An extensive page of links to privacy-related advocacy organizations, printed materials, and government agencies.

Pew Research Internet Project (www.pewinternet.org). The Pew Research Internet Project publishes extensive reports and studies dealing with many aspects of Internet use.

Privacy.org (www.privacy.org). A news and resource site jointly sponsored by the Electronic Privacy Information Center and Privacy International.

Privacy Rights Clearinghouse (www.privacyrights.org). Provides a wealth of discussion and documents pertaining to privacy issues related to government, online commerce, workplaces, and health.

Worlds of David Brin (www.davidbrin.com/transparency.html). A collection of Brin's published writings and blog posts on a wide variety of privacy-related topics.

Index

Note: Boldface page numbers indicate illustrations.